To Thomas Sowell

For fighting economic ignorance
with clarity and insight.

© 2024 The Tuttle Twins Holding Co.
All rights reserved.

No graphic, visual, electronic, film, microfilm, tape recording, or any other means may be used to reproduce in any form, without prior written permission of the author, except in the case of brief passages embodied in critical reviews and articles.

ISBN 979-8-88688-027-4

Boyack, Connor, author.
Stanfield, Elijah, illustrator; Stanfield, Cathryn, illustrator assistant.

The Tuttle Twins and the Medals of Merit / Connor Boyack.

Cover design by Elijah Stanfield
Edited and typeset by Connor Boyack

Printed in the United States

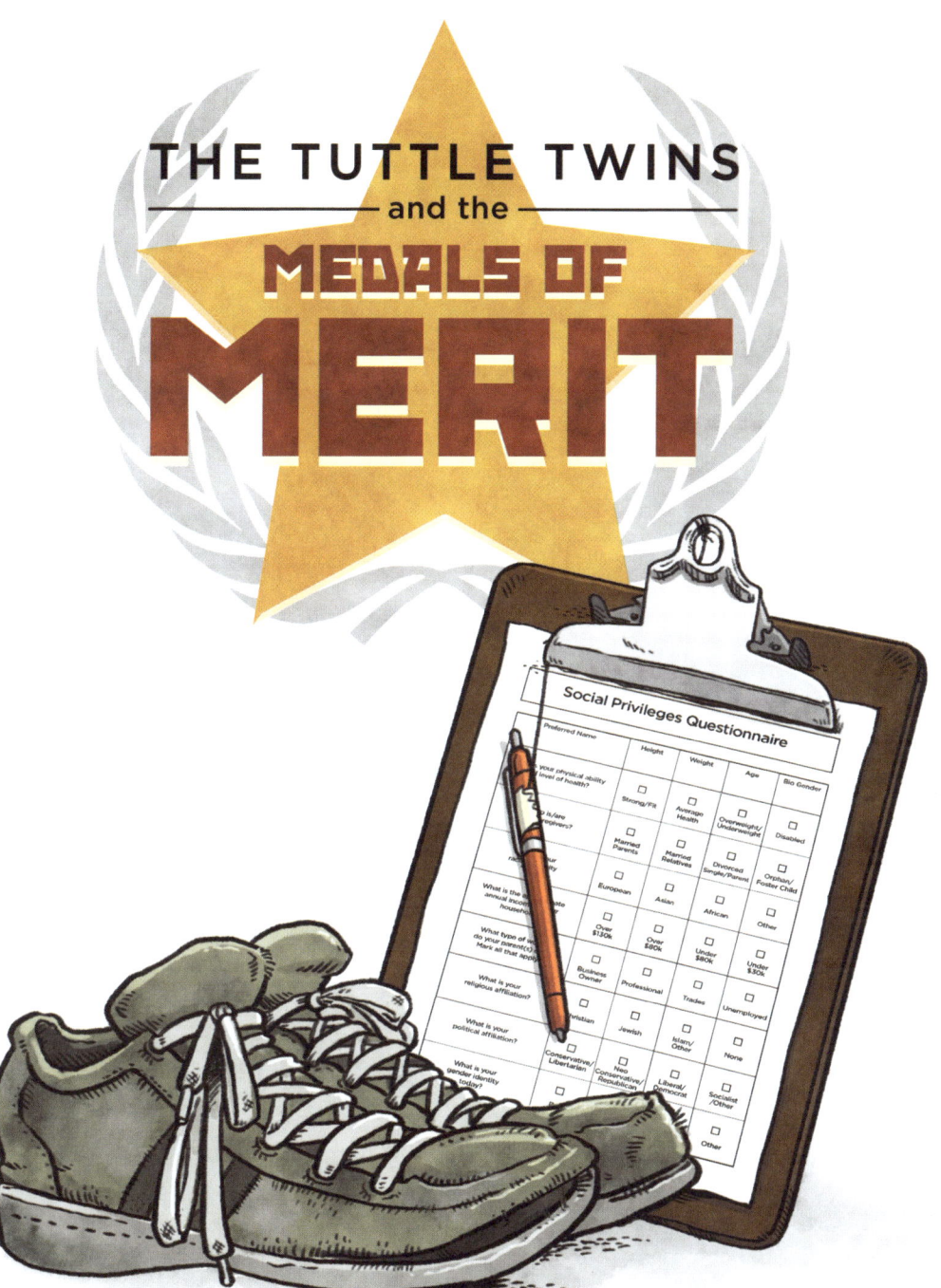

THE TUTTLE TWINS
and the
MEDALS OF MERIT

CONNOR BOYACK

Illustrated by Elijah Stanfield

Ethan Tuttle breathed out slowly as he began his hamstring stretch. He forced his mind to ignore the discomfort and focus on his goal to touch his toes.

He had never been very flexible. Emily, however, had been sitting in a full split for five minutes while she read her new comic book. "Show-off!" he teased.

"Isn't that what sports is all about?" Emily responded, smirking.

"I suppose," Ethan said. "Today, it's about bringing home some medals!" Their homeschool group had formed a track and field team, The Mighty Mustangs, and today was their first track meet.

Coach Eric had a simple motto: "Be great!" He had been conditioning the team with diet, form, and strength training, and running to the point of exhaustion. Strict discipline was required to perform to the best of their ability, he always said.

"In sports, it doesn't matter who you are, where you're from, or how much money you have," Coach Eric taught. "What matters is *merit*—the measurable results you achieve by being the strongest and fastest. It's a challenge to be the greatest you can be."

The sun blazed overhead but the air was cool. The energy was palpable as the teams filled the city track. Everyone was eager to test their skills and enjoy the events.

"We've been training so hard for this," Candace said in a huddle with the team. "I hope we get a chance to really show our stuff!"

"Oh, we will," a muscular boy named Javier replied. He was the most experienced member on the team and wanted to beat the record in the shot put.

"But hope and chance won't help us now," Javier said. "Today will only show the results of our work and preparation. Period."

A voice suddenly boomed, "Good afternoon, everyone!"

All eyes focused on the woman with the megaphone. "I'm Ms. Francis, your new sports director! But you can call me Taylor." She paused a moment and a few people hesitantly clapped.

"I was once on a track team like you," Taylor began. "But all the other kids were faster and stronger than me. My mom couldn't afford nice running shoes, gym memberships, or even good food like some of the other kids had. Their privileges gave them an advantage over me. So, I gave up." Taylor's voice choked on the words. Her childhood experience obviously still hurt her.

"Fast forward to today," she said. "I have a disabled daughter who would never know what it's like to be a winner because the system isn't fair. It rewards the strong and privileged. That changes now."

The twins exchanged a curious glance; how else would you judge a race other than by whoever was the fastest?

"This year," Taylor continued, "we're going to try something new—a credit system to ensure everyone is included and has an equal opportunity to win, no matter their life situation or skill level!" She held up a clipboard. "Before we start, each participant must fill out this questionnaire."

The kids all took clipboards. The questions started typically enough for a sports competition: age, height, and weight. But then there were some other ones that seemed odd: ethnicity, estimated family income, political affiliation, and gender identity.

Candace frowned. "Why would they need to know any of this for a track meet?!" she asked, reluctantly filling out the form.

As the event began, the initial competitive excitement was replaced with an air of confusion.

Emily was awarded second place in the high jump, losing to a boy who barely cleared three feet. She jumped five feet, eleven inches!

Javier came in third in the shot put, despite breaking the record. Both kids who beat him had never thrown before and didn't even come close to his distance.

And Ethan and his teammate Jaiden had similar experiences with the hurdles and long jump.

The relay race is where the team really shined. They crossed the finish line first! But then Taylor's shrill voice from the megaphone stole the victory. "The winner of the relay race is... Engels Elementary!"

Ethan was bewildered. "What? How? They have a girl in a wheelchair and came in dead last!"

"This doesn't seem fair!" Emily muttered, feeling dejected.

But when she looked up at the podium and saw the faces of Taylor's new winners, she had second thoughts. For the first time in their lives these kids were being treated like champions. Was that so bad? Maybe the new system really *was* more fair than the old. After all, a child's disadvantages are no fault of their own. They didn't ask for their family circumstances or physical disabilities.

After the winners received their medals, Taylor handed out ribbons to the other competitors with phrases like "I Care" or "I Won Because We Are One" printed on them.

Coach Eric was furious. "This new system does not inspire discipline or effort," he said pointedly.

"¡Afuera!" Javier shouted, throwing his ribbon to the ground. "I trained for a long time to break that record. Now I feel robbed!"

Several kids from other teams, standing nearby, began to nod. Taylor looked around nervously. "New rule!" she bellowed into her megaphone. "If you complain about the new system, that means you don't care about others and are selfish."

"It means you think you're better than the underprivileged. If you complain, you will lose 20 credits in the next competition!"

"Also, effective immediately, I'll be removing the trophies and plaques of past record holders. Those athletes won under the old system of inequality. They were never *real* champions."

Coach Eric clenched his jaw as decades of achievement were discarded. The twins and their teammates were not sure how to respond.

Training resumed on Monday morning. The teammates jogged in formation behind Coach Eric as he led them on a two-mile run to the park.

"My lungs are about to burst!" Jaiden groaned.

"What's the point of going through all this pain?" Ethan complained. "Merit doesn't win medals anymore."

When the team turned the corner, a line of police cars whizzed past with sirens blaring, heading toward the nearby college.

As they approached the campus, they saw hundreds of protesters chanting slogans outside the auditorium. The scene was chaotic.

"What's going on?" Emily wondered aloud.

After a few moments, Coach Eric snapped his fingers. "I think I know," he said, taking out his phone. He tapped on the screen to show a live video being broadcast of some protesters yelling at a man who had come to give a lecture.

"I used to be a Marxist, like you," the man said.

"Karl Marx thought that history is a story of the rich class ruling over the poor class," the man said, speaking over the shouting. "He imagined a new system of socialism to end inequality in the world. His theory was convincing to many!"

The chanting started to fade, making it easier to hear him. "But every society that has attempted to live by Marxist philosophies has found themselves in ruin and poverty. I want to tell you why."

The crowd roared with anger. "Sowell must not speak! Sowell must not speak!"

Police encircled the man to protect him from objects being thrown at him. As they headed toward his car to leave they passed more angry protesters. Emily spotted Taylor, fervently waving her own sign, which read "Diversity, Equity, Inclusion — Or Else!"

"You kids shouldn't stay here," Coach Eric said, telling his team to run ahead. "I understand now what Taylor is up to. I'll catch up with y'all in a bit."

At the park, the team gathered around the drinking fountain to wait. "So why should we go through the pain of training anymore?" Ethan asked again.

"Winning under this new system isn't about our abilities. Merit doesn't matter," Emily said, pulling a copy of Taylor's questionnaire from her pocket. "It's about how you answer the questions on *this*."

Candace suddenly had an idea. "Hey! We can answer this in a way that will give us bonus credits!" she deviously suggested. "I'll claim to be a blind immigrant from Timbuktu!"

Javier was stunned. "So we're going to play along and pretend to be disadvantaged?" he asked in disbelief. "Me, pretend to be a poor lightweight who can't throw?"

Just then a voice came from a car parked nearby. "Sometimes the best way to teach a truth is to point out the absurdity of the error." It was Thomas Sowell, the man from the protest. "But it might not be enough to fix your situation."

Mr. Sowell walked towards the team, wearing a tracksuit. Coach Eric followed, ready for practice!

"Mr. Sowell came to the college to speak, but those people were so afraid of what he might say that they used violence to stop him," Coach Eric said. "Good news is, that gives him time to speak to us!"

The kids were curious about what they saw and heard at the college and began asking a lot of questions.

"Why were they so angry at you?"

"Why didn't those protesters want you to speak?"

"Who's Karl Marx anyway?"

"You're in luck! That's exactly what I'm here to discuss," Mr. Sowell said. "But Coach Eric tells me that you've encountered a bit of Marxism already."

The group looked at each other, confused by how that could be. They'd never even heard of the word.

"*Marxism* is a philosophy developed by a notable thinker, Karl Marx. He lived 200 years ago," Mr. Sowell began. "He observed that history was filled with injustice and inequality—feudal kings dominating those who labored on their property."

Coach Eric blew his whistle and instructed the team to carry him across the field. "Oh great, now we have to work while we learn," Ethan said, straining to heft Coach Eric's leg over his shoulder.

Mr. Sowell walked beside the struggling kids. "Many were hopeful that the newly independent United States would end this struggle between classes of people, but Marx saw that it didn't. Others took the place of the king. They made the laws, owned the banks, controlled the land, and taxed the workers, who had to use their time and energy to make this new ruling class richer and richer, while they remained poor, just like before."

The team reached the end of the field and collapsed, exhausted by the weight of their coach.

"Well, that doesn't seem fair!" Candace insisted. "How did he plan to fix it?"

Mr. Sowell smiled. "Marx believed that *property* was to blame for this oppressive situation. He theorized that the struggle between classes would end when the workers took the property from the ruling class and used it to benefit all, equally. This is called *socialism*."

"Equality sounds great!" Ethan jumped onto Coach Eric's back. "Now, *you* march!" The others jumped on, forcing him to carry them all across the field.

"That's the spirit," Mr. Sowell chuckled. "Marx's ideas really meant that no one would be allowed to become greater than another."

"The oppressor is now the oppressed!" Candace yelled triumphantly, just as Coach Eric collapsed on the ground, bringing the whole team along with him.

"Eventually, Marx believed everyone would be equal, as socialism gave way to *communism*," Mr. Sowell said.

"Communism? I heard Grandpa say how horrible that was," Emily said. "But equality is good, right?"

"Not like this. Look at where you all are now," Mr. Sowell pointed to the pile of teammates. "When no one is allowed to be great, then everyone fails."

The whole team was twisted and bruised on the ground. This was obviously *not* the kind of equality anyone wanted.

"In every nation that adopts Marxism, forcing equality requires a government with total control," Coach Eric said as his team helped him up. "Violence is used to take property, to keep anyone from earning more, and to punish anyone who stands up to those in power."

"The communist dream of 'equality' that Marx wanted has always become a *totalitarian* nightmare of slavery and suffering," Mr. Sowell added.

"We heard you say that you used to believe in Marxism. What changed your mind?" Ethan asked.

Freedom to own property is the source of your opportunity and prosperity.

Freedom to earn the full reward of your work inspires greatness.

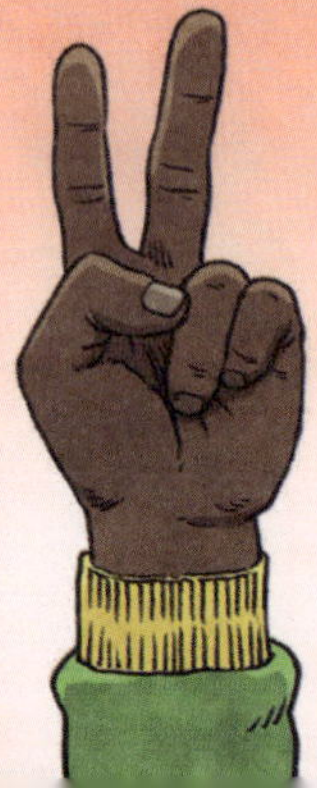

Freedom of choice reveal the true valu of your abiliti and product

"I realized three truths," Mr. Sowell said, holding up a finger. "First, property ownership is not to blame—it's actually the source of opportunity and prosperity. The real oppression was from the violent theft by the ruling class. They became rich because they took away the freedom to own property by force of law."

"So Marx had it backward all along," Javier said. "He wanted the government to steal property too, just like the old ruling class did, which doesn't help the poor at all."

Mr. Sowell nodded, holding up another finger. "Second, under forced equality, no one reaches their full potential. The freedom to earn the full rewards of our work is what drives us to be our best selves."

"Realize this: none of you are equal," he added, holding up a third finger. "We are each unique individuals with different abilities and preferences. So we can't have equal lives, but everyone *should* be equally free to make different choices for their life. That's how we can discover the true value of our own abilities. *That's* the truth."

The team let out a loud cheer in agreement with Mr. Sowell. "I think speaking to you all was a better use of my time than anything I could have done at that sorry excuse for a college," he said.

"Wait, didn't this have something to do with us?" Emily wondered. "You said we already encountered Marxism. Where?"

"Don't you see?" Javier asked. "Taylor has turned our track meet into a Marxist disaster. She's trying to force everyone to be equal, and saying that great athletes don't deserve to be rewarded."

Coach Eric nodded. "Like Mr. Sowell said, Marx's followers once saw property as the cause of inequality. But today's Marxists want to change *any* system where some people have an advantage."

EQUITY: CONTROLLED OUTCOME OF REWARDS

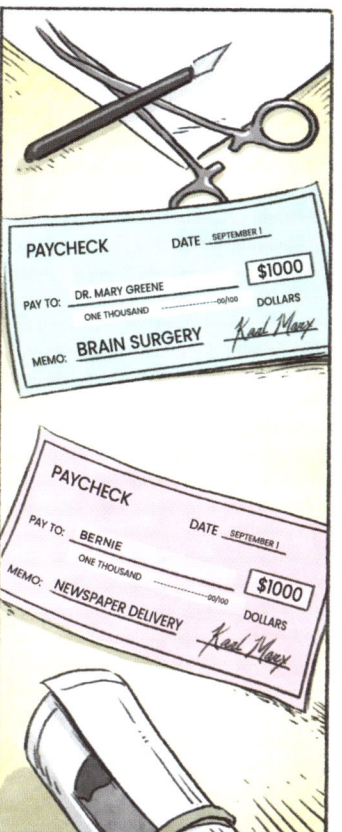

"They want equal outcomes in education, sports, and employment, regardless of merit. Guaranteeing outcomes isn't equality—this is called *equity*."

"But that just makes everyone equal losers!" Ethan said. "Mr. Sowell realized the lie of Marxism by learning the truth. So we need to teach everyone that Taylor's Marxist system is a lie, too."

Mr. Sowell offered to help the team devise a plan.

Saturday brought a new track meet, and the twins' spirits were sunny like the weather. They had a plan!

"Remember," Coach Eric said as the team entered the field. "In a Marxist system, your weakness *may* get you bonus points, but free people strive to be the best they can be, no matter their circumstances." He huddled the team into a circle, where they put their hands together.

"One... two... three..."

"BE GREAT!" the team shouted in unison.

"Merit Majority?" Taylor shouted over a megaphone.

"That's us!" Coach Eric said. The team ran to Taylor while he marched to the sidelines, armed with a clipboard, measuring tape, and stopwatch.

"We changed our team name," Javier said to some other athletes, "because we think the majority of people want to be recognized for their abilities, not for their disabilities. Who's with us?"

Taylor heard Javier's comment. "You, young person, just lost 20 credits for *each* member of your team!" she said loudly in a megaphone for all to hear. Then she scribbled dramatically on her clipboard.

After that, other athletes avoided the Merit Majority team for fear of losing credits too. To make things worse, the twins noticed that many of them were doing what Candace had first thought to do—filling out their handicap questionnaires with imaginary answers that would give them bonus points. The team's sunny disposition gave way to gloom.

"Mr. Sowell was right," Emily said, holding back tears. "Playing Taylor's game won't teach anyone anything. Everyone is just validating her system even more. No one wants to stand with us."

"Remember the plan," Ethan said resolutely. "The best way to fight Marxism is to resist its lies, even if it seems unpopular. People will slowly rally around the truth, and the scales will eventually tip our way."

The team wanted to trust the plan, but for the time being, they had never felt so powerless and alone!

In spite of the opposition, Merit Majority competed in all their events with enthusiasm. They ran, jumped, and threw to the very best of their abilities, while Coach Eric recorded times and distances.

Javier even broke the shot put record, again! But no matter the outcome of the contests, the medals went to others. This was expected, but what was surprising was that no one was smiling this time— not even the kids who got the awards. Only Taylor seemed to feel pleased with herself.

"Excuse me?" a girl asked, approaching the Merit Majority team in her wheelchair. They gathered around to listen. "I've always wished I could be a track star, but my disability makes that impossible. So when I learned I could still win with new rules, I was excited!"

She held up her new gold medal, tears welling in her eyes. "But this? This is actually embarrassing. I don't want to be rewarded for my disabilities," she added. "I have an idea to help you change the system back, so that my *real* abilities are rewarded."

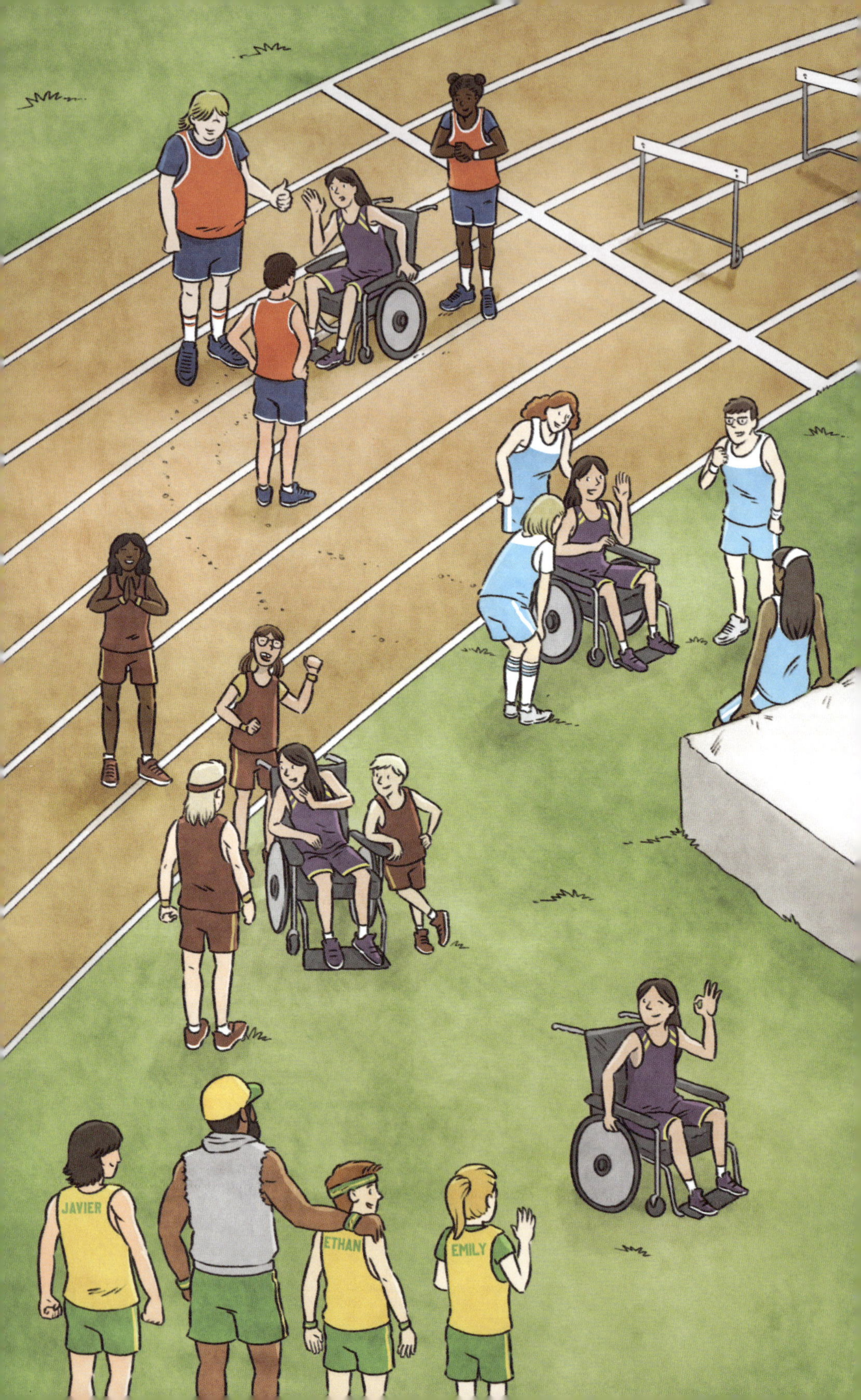
JAVIER
ETHAN
EMILY

The team relay race, the final event, would take place after the lunch break; they didn't have much time. While the Merit Majority team worked on their part of the plan, their new ally, Beth, wheeled from team to team, explaining the secret details of what would happen next. To her surprise, not one team objected to it. Everyone was now ready to participate in a revolt against Taylor's absurd Marxist system.

"You see? Taylor might not want to handle reality, but truth is popular!" Coach Eric reassured them, looking proudly at his team. "The majority just needed a few brave kids to lead the way."

He looked around the track at all the young, hopeful faces. For the first time that day, everyone was smiling and eager for a real contest of ability. "True greatness comes when everyone is encouraged to succeed by their own effort and individual talent— by their own merit," he told his team. "Not through special treatment. One more event… let's be great!"

The megaphone blasted. "Runners to their places!"

Ethan, Emily, Jaiden, and Candace approached the starting line for the relay race. The energy felt electric. When Taylor's whistle cut the air, the first group of runners shot off the blocks like bullets.

Emily was fast—very fast. Weeks of Coach Eric's intense regiment of flexibility, strength, and form training had paid off. Her legs snapped back and forth so quickly, she felt like her toes hardly touched the ground. She was flying!

In her peripheral view, she saw the other runners fall behind. Soon she couldn't even hear the sounds of their steps, only the gasps of amazement from her parents as she passed them. She approached the relay zone far ahead of the others. Her baton rose toward Ethan, who waited with his hand out.

Soon, Beth's plan would go into effect, and Taylor would get a lesson on what diversity, equity, and inclusion looked like in the real world.

In a flurry of activity, each team's coach crossed the sidelines, carrying small equipment dollies and straps. They harnessed up the next group of runners like horses for a chariot race.

"What is going on?!" Taylor shrieked.

Ethan snatched the baton from Emily, who then mounted the makeshift chariot. He trudged forward on the next leg of the race, but the lead that Emily had gained for Merit Majority closed steadily.

Copernicus, a heavy-set boy from Spoonerville Elementary, had been the slowest kid at the meet, finishing last in every event. But Beth's new rules didn't give special treatment for his weakness—it instead highlighted his own greatness. He pulled his chariot with ease, while Ethan struggled. The crowd roared with real enthusiasm—not the phony applause the kids received for winning Marxist medals earlier that day.

By the end of the leg, Spoonerville's team was neck and neck with Merit Majority!

Rounding the corner, Ethan slapped the baton into Jaiden's hand. He bounded like a gazelle evading a pack of lions. His long legs were perfect for leaping effortlessly over the hurdles, which on any other day would have guaranteed him a victory.

Except jumping *over* things wasn't the goal in this new contest. When the racers approached the long lines of hurdles on the track, they instead dropped to their hands to crawl *under* them! All, that is, except a boy named Donny.

It was likely impossible for Donny, a little person from Meadowbrook Academy, to ever jump over those hurdles. But he was angry that his dwarfism was recognized as a handicap in Taylor's system.

He ran with ease under the hurdles, soon taking the lead. "Donny's privilege puts the others at a disadvantage, don't you think?" the Meadowbrook coach teased Taylor.

The crowd cheered for Donny.

Mr. Sowell had been working on a surprise for the awards ceremony while observing the whole spectacle unfold from beside the bleachers. "Clever educational presentation," Mr. Sowell said to Coach Eric, who was grinning from ear to ear.

"They're just putting the principles you taught them into action," Coach Eric reminded him.

Mr. Sowell nodded, pleased that a new generation was rejecting the blunder of Marxism and recognizing the value of their own unique abilities.

For the final leg of the relay race, Beth wheeled herself onto the track, followed by Candace and the other racers... also in wheelchairs!

"Instead of thinking like a victim, I turned my challenge into a strength," Beth explained to Candace, who cheered her on.

"Don't think I'm going to go easy on you," Candace smiled, waiting for the baton. "Greatness is only achieved when everyone works to be the best that they can be. I'll see you at the finish line."

"Get ready to eat my dust!" Beth shot back.

The volume of the crowd reached ear-splitting levels when Donny relayed the baton to his final teammate. Meadowbrook Academy had pulled so far into the lead that by the time Candace and Beth got their batons, they had a lot of catching up to do.

The friendly rivalry dissolved from their minds as their intense focus turned inward. The only thing left was the reality of their beating hearts and the pain in their hands as they spun their wheels. Their arms moved like two machines in perfect unison. Locked in at a high-speed pace, they both soon passed the leader with only a dozen meters left to go.

"Be great!" bellowed Coach Eric from the sideline.

"Go Beth! You can win, sweetie!" The words came from a voice that no one expected. Taylor, whose face was wet with tears, was jumping up and down with excitement. "My daughter *is* great!"

When the two wheelchairs blurred through the finish line ribbon, no one noticed the winner. All eyes were on the scene of a child who had just proven her own true greatness to her mother. "I'm sorry, Mom. But I didn't want to win with fake credits—I wanted to earn it and win for real."

"You're right, Beth. I was just trying to make it fair, but you are amazing and strong without my help!"

"Listen up, everybody!" Ethan shouted into the megaphone, trying to quiet the crowd. "Now it's time for the grand finale. The medals ceremony!"

The crowd erupted into cheers. Tensions eased, and the air was filled with a sense of justice being restored.

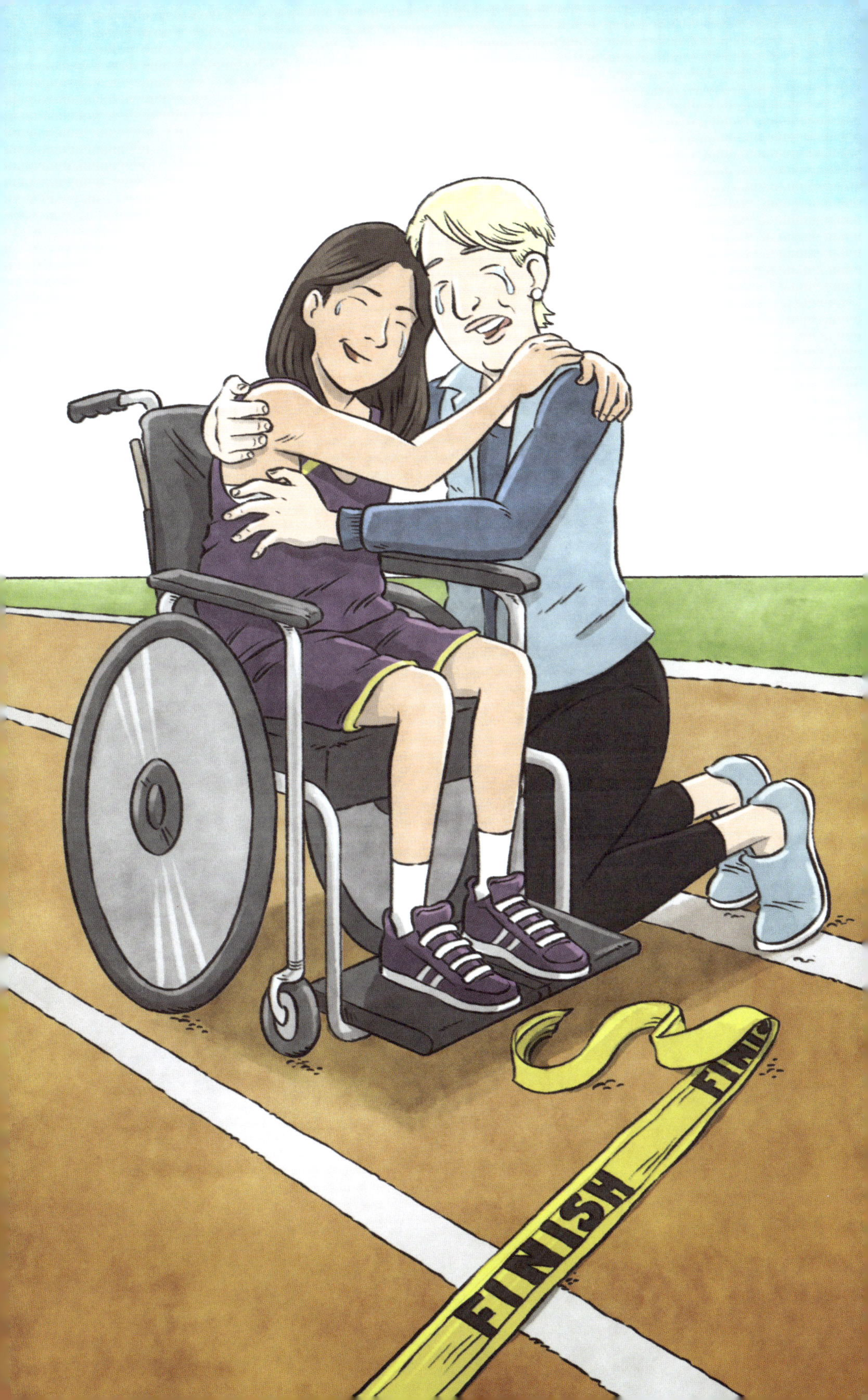
FINI
FINISH

MERIT MATTERS

The setting sun cast a warm glow over the field as the teams and spectators gathered at the winner's podium. Draped above it was Mr. Sowell's surprise project—a banner which read "Merit Matters," made from Taylor's discarded ribbons.

Throughout the day Coach Eric had documented the results of each event, and so medals were re-awarded to the deserved winners. And Javier's shot put score was added to the plaque of records.

"What about the winners of the relay race?" Beth asked, eagerly. "Who finished first?"

A video taken from a parent's phone showed that Merit Majority had won, fair and square. Taylor's eyes sank. She wanted her daughter to win so badly. "Maybe we could use the credits… just one more time?" she suggested.

"I was hoping our team would win, but we didn't. This belongs to the real winners," Beth said, presenting the medal to Candace. "They earned it."

"You taught me quite a lesson," Taylor remarked, looking at Beth. "When I tried to force everyone to be equal, it diminished the value of our differences, and the joy of achieving something you earned yourself. When that's taken away, I guess it's not just the winners who lose. Everyone does."

Emily put her hand on Beth. "Greatness isn't always recognized with medals and plaques, but what you learned today definitely is great!"

"And worthy of merit!" Ethan added, appearing from behind Beth, cloaking her in the banner of ribbons, making a long cape. The crowd hoisted Beth and Taylor into the air, cheering.

The twins exchanged a proud look, knowing they had stood up for what was true and tipped the scales back to reality.

The End

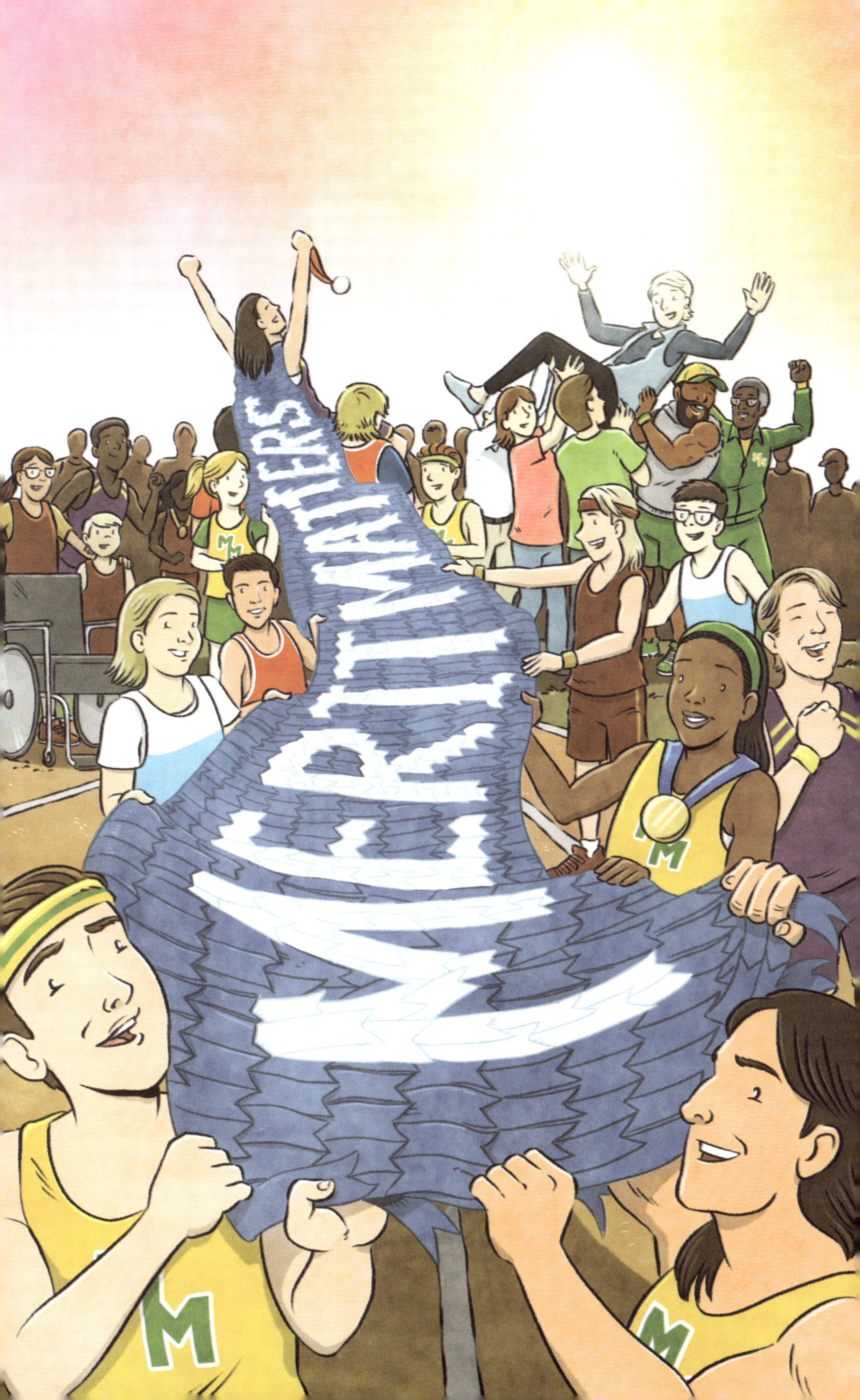
MERIT MATTERS

Karl Marx called for a classless society with communal ownership of production—abolishing private property, which he saw as the source of inequality. His ideas inspired various communist regimes like the Soviet Union and Maoist China, which led to brutal repression, widespread economic failure, and tens of millions of deaths.

When implemented, Marx's ideas have resulted in totalitarianism and immense suffering, demonstrating the catastrophic consequences of his theories. And yet, many people today hold political views that have their foundation in Marx's ideas of struggle between societal classes.

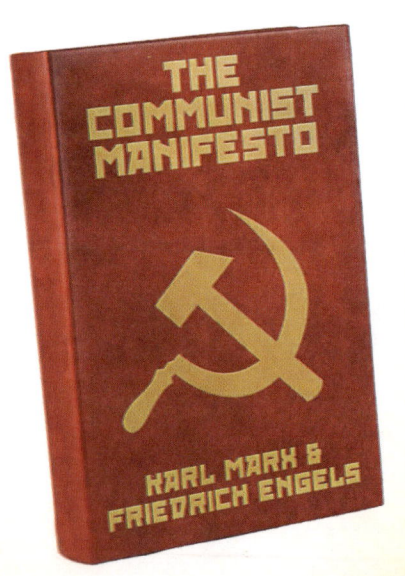

"The history of all hitherto existing society is the history of class struggles... The theory of Communism may be summed up in the single sentence: Abolition of private property."

—Karl Marx

Thomas Sowell, in his book *Marxism: Philosophy and Economics*, explores Marx's theories, their historical context, and their practical impacts, arguing that Marxism's promises of equality and prosperity fail in reality, leading instead to economic inefficiency and totalitarianism.

Hans-Hermann Hoppe's book *A Theory Of Socialism And Capitalism* offers a devastating critique of Marx's ideas, pointing out that interfering with private property rights and market processes—individuals freely choosing and acting—leads to inefficiencies and impoverishment.

Ludwig von Mises is widley considered the most notable free market economist. His book *Socialism: An Economic and Sociological Analysis* illustrates how socialism's promise of equality is unattainable, ultimately reducing everyone's standard of living and leading to poorer outcomes.

The Author

Connor Boyack is president of Libertas Institute, a free market think tank in Utah. In that capacity he has changed a significant number of laws in favor of personal freedom and free markets, and has launched a variety of educational projects, including The Tuttle Twins children's book series. Connor is the author of over 40 books.

A California native and Brigham Young University graduate, Connor currently resides in Lehi, Utah, with his wife and two children.

The Illustrator

Elijah Stanfield is owner of Red House Creative, a media production company.

A longtime student of Austrian economics, history, and the classical liberal philosophy, Elijah has dedicated much of his time and energy to promoting the ideas of free markets and individual liberty. Some of his more notable works include producing eight videos in support of Ron Paul's 2012 presidential candidacy. He currently resides near Nashville, Tennessee, with his wife April and their six children.

Contact us at TuttleTwins.com!

Glossary of Terms

Communism: A system where the government owns all property and makes all decisions about who gets what.

Equity: An attempt to create fairness by giving special treatment to those who see themselves as underprivileged or deserving of special benefits.

Marxism: A set of ideas, promoted by Karl Marx, where those who see themselves as victims believe they should be given what those who are "privileged" have.

Merit: Earning something because of your skills, effort, and achievements.

Socialism: A system in which property is taken from those who earned it in order to be redistributed to other who did not.

Totalitarian: A government where one person or a small group has total control over every part of people's lives.

Discussion Questions

1. Why should we celebrate and reward merit?
2. How might rewarding everyone equally, regardless of effort or achievement, impact motivation and personal growth?
3. How does the concept of "equity" differ from "equality"?
4. What are true examples of things happening in our world that are like the Marxist Track Meet?
5. How does striving to be the best you can be benefit individuals and society as a whole?

Don't Forget the Activity Workbook!

Visit **TuttleTwins.com/MeritWorkbook** to download the PDF and provide your children with all sorts of activities to reinforce the lessons they learned in the book!